Fighting
for
Joy

DEB LUIKEN

Table of Contents

Preface

A re you feeling buried, depressed, and overloaded? Then this book is for you. I truly believe no matter how bad things look right now, you can get over what is dragging you down and get happy, again. You have the power to take it back. The choice is yours, to regain your happiness, again.

You probably don't even realize the garbage you have allowed people to dump on you. The only way we can get out from underneath all this garbage is by forgiving everyone everything.

Ephesians 4:31-32 Get rid of all bitterness, rage and anger, brawling and slander, along with every form of malice. Be kind and compassionate to one another, forgiving each other, just as in Christ, God forgave *you.*

How many of us have grudges and unforgiveness we have held since our childhood? Aah ...all of us.

If *you* are reading *this book than you* are ready to do some major cleaning in your mind. You are ready to release the trash that people have dumped on you. All this unforgiveness is *causing* heart disease, obesity, cancer, and all other types of diseases too numerous to mention.

I am going to tell you why you need to forgive these people. Well, it is hurting you and not them. I will show you easier ways to let the hurt go. And I will help you to forgive these people for their errors and maybe even show them love and compassion. By doing all of this, you will be regaining a life that is truly worth living again.

Life is to be enjoyed not endured.

Chapter 1

Forgiving Others

I'm going to tell you that there are many people that just don't have a screen from their brain to their mouth.

We allow them to ruin our day. We tell others what this or that person said. We repeat it in our heads until we even believe what they said.

Believe it or not, there are many, many people without *a* screen and we run into them daily. On top of all that we have bad drivers out there, always getting in our way. We don't even need to have a conversation with people and we allow them to ruin our day.

Now I'm going to tell you a little something. These people just keep going through their lives, not giving another thought to you. They get up every morning *enjoying their lives* and *not even caring how you feel.* Those dirty scoundrels *don't even care about you.*

WHAT!! How dare they! They took your joy, they took *your peace,* and they don't care. There are people that just don't have a lot of compassion for one another. Or, they are hurting so much they can't realize they are hurting others. We cannot allow these people to hurt us another day. Or allow them to steal our dreams from our lives.

So, the only person we can deal with is ourselves. It might be everyone else's fault. But we can't stop them from how they act. We can only work on ourselves.

Trust me I have tried to fix my friends, and my family, to no avail. Total waste of my energy. Tried to fix men. Why don't they just get it, already?

ARG!!

People are who they are. Then God showed us this in verse Matthew 7:3, "And why worry about a speck in your friends eye when you have log in your own."

WHAT!!! ME!! NOOO!!!!

UMM...

So, dear Lord, what is my plank?

UNFORGIVENESS! I heard him plain as day.

Why do I have to forgive them? They are the ones who did... Well, the list is endless. They have the plank, not me. I'm nice. I'm *caring.* I'm *loving.* But, I am *also* very *bitter.*

Let me just tell you, people have trampled me. And they *did not deserve forgiveness.*

So, there I sat with all my anger, bitterness, self-righteousness, and self-pity (well-deserved self-pity, if I may add).

Miles and miles of anger. Piles of self-pity. Even if they did apologize, I probably wouldn't have heard it through my thick skull. That's when I realized, *people are going on with their lives.* And, I'm stuck, stuck in *piles of trash* that belonged to someone else. So how do we get *unstuck?* It starts a little at a time.

"GOD IS OUR REFUGE AND STRENGTH A VERY PRESENT HELP IN TROUBLE," PSALM 46:1.

I always start with prayer. God is the great healer. Ask God for guidance, ask for His presence in your work to heal. And ask for a loving and forgiving heart.

Find a nice quiet, comfortable place. Take a deep relaxing breath. Close your eyes. Picture the person who buried your joy. Find a way in your heart to forgive that person. Put your hand on your heart. Take another deep breath. Have compassion.

You have no idea what that person has gone through. Ask God to bless that person. When we ask this of God, it's to have God work in their lives. We are asking God to handle the situation. Trust God. Ask God to work in your own heart as well as theirs.

Next, I want *you* to picture your hurt. What does it look like? What does it feel I like? Do you want it inside of you? Take another deep breath. (Breathing scans your body *and* tells your brain and your heart what's going on.) This will help in the process. Now ask yourself do you want to keep these feelings in your body. They are truly destroying you. So let's just pack them up. Bag them up. Sometimes, I see Jesus ready to take them from me. Or I picture putting them in the trash outside. Sometimes, I picture all the hurtful words, lying all over the place, and I vacuum them up. Just let it go. Take another deep breath and see how you feel. This process does take some time, if you feel you are getting stuck, take more deep relaxing breaths. Your Heavenly Father is always there to assist you. You have probably been carrying this heaviness for quite some time, and it might take more than one attempt to free yourself from it.

You will have to go through this individually with everyone that has hurt you in any way. You probably won't want to do everyone all at once. Give yourself time between each person. You will feel relief even after working on just one person. You will know when to release another.

God never wanted us to get buried.

That is why he said in Ephesians 4:26, "Don't let the sun go down on your anger. It gets a strong foot hold and starts to destroy your peace in life."

It starts to get your health and it is harder now to get rid of and makes it easier to get angry at others and before you know it you are buried. You now believe you have a right to be angry. You now have heart disease, depression or any number of illnesses. And now it's hard to handle just everyday problems and you start inflicting people with your anger. Then we become a society full of angry people full of road rage, entitlement and self-righteousness. Who wants to live in that world?

Now as we unbury ourselves and forgive everyone, everything, somehow the world around you will change. The people you have forgiven and got rid of their garbage they gave you will affect them also. Somehow they know, without even saying a word to them, they know. They know they can't treat you like they once had. Dumping their garbage on you, and if they still do dump their garbage on you. You won't be so willing to accept it and keep it for decades. You will now recognize this does not belong to you. Picture yourself giving it back to them or to the big dumpster outside. Jesus' hands are always ready to help you find your way back to your life that God destined you to have. And don't forget to *breathe*. This always helps to think clearer and release.

The next step is to release these people. Take nice deep breaths, get really relaxed, close your eyes. Picture the person who hurt you.

You no longer are accepting their garbage in your life. You have cleaned it all out. But you are still emotionally attached to this person. Look to see if you have cords running from you to them. Then they are still taking your energy, your joy and your destiny.

The cords can be cut, pulled out, or untangled. I usually find this is not an easy step. It requires visualization, a bit of concentration, and lots of deep breaths. People we love have hurt us to the core; we have held onto this for a long time, and it is very intertwined in our hearts. Releasing people is very powerful. It frees you, and them. Even though this step is hard, I know you can do it. Don't give up until you have released every cord attached to you, and them. Use wire cutters if you need to. And don't forget about the assistance of God. He is always ready to help.

Chapter 2

The Hard Stuff

What about the really hard stuff? Like divorce, rape, loss of a child, abuse.

There are monsters out there passing *as* people. They are inflicting their ugliness on the human race in unimaginable ways.

Do we have to forgive them?

Yes! Yes, we do. I can feel the heaviness in all your chests. I know this is hard. Really hard. They do not deserve this kindness, for hurting you to your core, every cell of your body has been affected. I know how you feel. I've been through my share of monsters. But listen to me this is not about them; this is about you.

You cannot enjoy your life until you let these monsters go. And the only way they go away is by forgiveness. You can do this. I know you can. If I can, so can you.

Make space in your day for this. It is just a memory; it can't hurt you any more than it does right now.

You do not have to be face to face with this person. You can do this right from your own living room.

Start by writing them a letter. Tell them all your feelings. Get it out. Just let it pour through you to the paper. I don't care if you can only scribble circles. Just release some anger on the paper.

When you are done with that part, write a BUT... I forgive you. I will not allow you to take my joy another minute of my day.

Don't forget to *breathe!* Close your eyes. Picture all your pain, *all* of your hurt, all your anger.

Bag it up. Box it up. Clean it up. Give it back to them, put it in the trash bin outside, *or* hand it off to Jesus. Take a deep breath and let it go.

Now, forgiving these people doesn't mean you have to hang around the, or bring them presents. No, it just means they don't have the right to hurt you anymore.

Take your power back. Like I said before, these people are going on with their lives not giving a second thought about you. So let it go. Let your anger and depression go. You allowed them to steal your joy from you. And you can take it back.

The only way to regain your power is through forgiveness.

Trust me! I have tried other ways. They just don't work. This does.

Listen, folks; you have literally taken all the people who have hurt your feelings, broken your heart. People have been total jerks to you. You are taking them everywhere. You take them out with friends, on vacation, to work with you. You take them home with you every night. You even bring them into second and third marriages.

They are strapped around your neck, choking you. They are strapped around your waist, ruining your digestive track. You have them strapped to your back. DO NOT take these people one more place with you.

How do you even get out of bed in the morning?

No wonder so many people are on antidepressants, just to get through the day.

Trust me; you are killing yourself a slow, painful, death by not forgiving.

Let the vengeance be God's.

People Wake Up!! By not forgiving them it is only destroying you. Romans 12:19, "Let him convict them. It is His to avenge, He will repay."

He's up anyway. And he can handle the situation so much better than you can. And by letting God handle it, you are taking the high road.

Take your joy back. You are the only one that can do it. Take the first step and ask God to avenge. Let God repay beauty for ashes.

Isaiah 61:3, " **God will** *restore beauty for your ashes, the* **oil of** *joy for your mourning, that they be made trees of righteousness, the planting of the* **Lord** *that He might be glorified."*

Don't forget to cut the cords between you and your monster. I am sure you do not want to be connected to this person in any way. This will help you to feel the power you have inside of you. Remember you can be pitiful or powerful, but you can't be both.

Chapter 3

Forgiving Yourself

If you think forgiving others is tough, for some reason forgiving ourselves is super hard. Our big fat egos get in the way.

Romans 3:23, "For all have sinned and fall short of the Glory of God." Mathew *12:31* Tells *us* that the only sin that is not forgiven is Blasphemy *against* the Spirit. All else is forgiven.

If God is willing to forgive you, then why then can you not forgive yourself? And maybe it is time to reread the Gospels. Jesus died a horrible death for all our sins. Once for all time! It is a disgrace to Jesus, hanging on to unforgiveness. We don't want to disgrace Jesus. *So* let's let it all go. And by hanging on to our sins, we cannot live the life we are destined to live. We have such a short time on this planet, and so much to do like have fun, enjoy life, and make a difference, even if it is in just one person. This is a really cool beautiful place to live; we can't truly enjoy it if we are hanging on to things of our past.

Just remember everyone on this planet has done things wrong. You are not alone. Picture your older self talking to your younger self. What would you like to say to the younger you. Be kind. Be gentle. It's time, my friend, to lift this heavy burden off of you.

Look at all the garbage you are creating for yourself. Look at the filth of your unforgiveness. This is doing no one any good to hang on to this hurt. You will never be strong enough to carry this, and live a successful life.

So, let's hand it to the hands, with the holes in the wrists. He has already paid the full price for your sins. He paid for them, and they belong to him. He has been waiting a long time for you to let it *go.*

Be kind to yourself. Learn to love yourself. God made you! Figure out all the good things God instilled in you. He made you for a reason. *He loves you.* By not liking yourself, you are insulting your Heavenly Father. Just remember, he knew every stupid thing you would ever do before he made you. And, *he chose to make anyway.*

So, sit comfortable, take deep breaths. Forgive yourself just like you would forgive your own best friend. Hand your garbage off to Jesus and remember what He has done for us. Thank Him for what He has done for you. Praise Him.

When you have done all that, find a paper and pen. Write down everything that is unique, awesome and amazing about you.

God has made each one of us for a special purpose.

Psalm 139:13 *& 14* - You alone created my inner being. You knitted me together inside my mother. I will give thanks to You because I have been so amazingly and miraculously made. Your works are miraculous and my soul is fully aware of this.

Isaiah 64:8 Yet you, Lord, are our Father. We are the clay. You are the potter. We are all the work of your hand.

Jeremiah 29:11 (one of my favorites) For I know the plans I have for you says the Lord. Plans to prosper you, not to harm you, plans to give you hope and a future.

And of course Romans 8:28 All things work for good for most who truly seek and love the Lord.

So release the things from your life that isn't prosperous, let go of the garbage. Fall in love with what God has made, and let God decide your future.

Chapter 4

Forgiving God

I've heard people say that God doesn't give us more than we can handle, but that is not how the Scripture reads, I Corinthians 10:13, "God is faithful, he will not let you be tempted more than you can bear, but when you are tempted he will also provide a way out."

He will not let you be tempted more than you can handle. Not the same thing at all. He gives us way more than we can handle.

For you mothers and fathers that have lost a child, you know you have been given way more than you can handle, or fighting cancer, been raped, those are all really super hard things to handle. God allows bad things to happen to us, and I would say without God there is very little healing. God is the only one who can help you through it.

John 10:10 says - The thief comes to steal, kill and destroy. I have come that they may have life and that they may have it abundantly.

Romans 8:28 says - and we know all things work together for good to those who love God, to those who are called according to his purpose. This is one of my favorite scriptures. It works for a lot of things in life.

You can do all things in Christ who strengthens you.

So, what I'm trying to tell you is God is very loving and kind; it's the thief that is destroying us. Satan knows how to pull you away from God. He knows every button to push. God, our Heavenly Father, knows your pain. He keeps track of all our sorrows. Psalms 56:8. Ask God to be gracious to you. He really does love you. He is about the one and only that can help you heal from this. He can turn your loss into a blessing. He can restore you better than before your loss.

If you remain in hate, you will destroy your life even more than it has been done. I know it's hard to let go of the heartache you are feeling. But, if you are reading this book, I know you will want to heal. We all want to feel Joy and Love, again.

Your Heavenly Father is always right there. He is waiting for you. His arms are wide open to help you, to regain your strength that the enemy took away.

We are to be thankful for all things. Even the trials and heartaches! First Thessalonians 5:18 I know this stings a little maybe even a lot. Forcing this thankfulness out of you will bring about healing, it's showing trust in God.

Jeremiah 29:11 says - We don't know the plans he has for us. Plans to prosper us.

By blaming God, we just won't heal, we will stay stuck in our sorrow. By taking God's hand and by putting trust in him you can get on top of it. You can get to a place where it's not controlling you, but healing you.

Remember to breathe. Nice cleansing breaths and run into God's arms.

There is no better way to make the enemy mad. The enemy that tried to destroy you.

I hope this book helps you to live a more joyful life with less clutter in your mind and body. To think clearer.

Don't let others steal your joy, but if they do, I hope you will recognize it quicker now, so you can take it back.

When you find your mind thinking about hurtful things, do these steps. Don't hang on to it. Take some deep breaths, and change your mind. Think about something else.

Did you know you have control over your mind? Yes, you do. All you have to do is think about something more cheerful. Don't let your mind control you. You control your mind. Everyone on this earth has gone through rough things. No one has escaped heartache.

I feel the secret to life's happiness is forgiveness.

Life is to be enjoyed, not endured. Yes, we go through hard times, but they just don't stay stuck. Take time to grieve. For everyone this is a different time frame. But when you feel it leaving, let it go. Be free. Get back to the things you enjoy.

Chapter 5

Learn to love yourself

Hopefully, you have completed the steps in this book. If you're still not feeling happy things are still getting you down a bit. Then maybe you need to learn to love yourself. I'm not talking about having a big ego and talking about yourself non-stop. We all know people like that. I'm talking about truly liking who you are, enjoying your own company. Trust me. You have an endless list of assists.

Now would be the time to start showing yourself all the things that make you a really unique individual. Not like anyone else.

So here is some homework for you to do. Buy a journal. Write a list of everything that makes you pretty cool. You can list your achievements, your creative talents, your abilities to get things done. Maybe you could ask a good friend what they like about you.

Sometimes we are so busy with life and seeing what everyone else is doing and what they are good at, that we can't see what we are really good at.

If we don't love ourselves, we won't respect ourselves. And if we don't love and respect ourselves, how can we expect anyone to love or respect us?

If you find yourself saying bad things about yourself in your, head or to others, this has to stop, immediately. If you can't be nice to yourself, how do you expect others to?

We teach people how to treat us. If we are saying things like, "I'm so dumb," or "I'm so fat." The people around us can sense this. So, be kind to yourself. When you hear yourself saying something negative, take a deep breath, and change it. Change your inner dialogue. Be your own best friend, and you will discover others being kinder to you. We all want to live in a world that is nicer and kinder. Let it start with you.

So take good care of yourself. Eat right, get some exercise, or go for walks. Spend time with friends.

Made in the USA
Middletown, DE
30 August 2019